Prague Travel Guide:

The Ultimate Prague, Czech Republic Tourist Trip Travel Guide

By

Angela Pierce

Table of Contents

Introduction 5

Chapter 1. Perfect Time to Visit The City of Prague 7

Chapter 2. City Culture... 9

Chapter 3. Food 10

Chapter 4. Night Life 12

Chapter 5. Experience The City of Prague 13

    The Best Attractions of Prague 13

Chapter 6. Shopping in The City... 23

Chapter 7. Places to Stay 25

Final Words 27

Thank You Page.. 30

Prague Travel Guide: The Ultimate Prague, Czech Republic Tourist Trip Travel Guide

By Angela Pierce

© Copyright 2015 Angela Pierce

Reproduction or translation of any part of this work beyond that permitted by section 107 or 108 of the 1976 United States Copyright Act without permission of the copyright owner is unlawful. Requests for permission or further information should be addressed to the author.

This publication is designed to provide accurate and authoritative information in regard to the subject matter covered. This work is sold with the understanding that the publisher is not engaged in rendering legal, accounting, or other professional services. If legal advice or other expert assistance is required, the services of a competent professional person should be sought.

First Published, 2015

Printed in the United States of America

Introduction

The great city of Europe, which is the second largest of the continent and is one of the best looking cities with outstanding beauties and some decent towers. The city of Prague has the best looking features and that is the reason why most of travelers, who are travelling through Europe, never miss to visit the place. The city is regarded as one of the best cities of the continent and it is one of the foremost places where most of the travelers visit and enjoy the beauty of the old Bohemian rich culture out there. The city has immense historical importance and it is one of the top places located at the side of the Vltava River. The most important thing that the travelers look for in the city is the historical pledge in the city that is there since 9th century. The city has been the place for the expansion of the Bohemians and it has been destroyed to a great extent during World War II. The perfect beauty of the city that was there before the WWII is not there anymore, yet the castles that are still there and the golden towers represent the rich culture that the city had in the past. The culture of the city is rich with great traditional and modern art and musical concerts. The traditional culture is so rich that the modern culture, although so improved cannot touch the valor of the city that was before. The city is full of energy and that makes the traveler love the place and find a great lot of energy in the city.

Chapter 1. Perfect Time to Visit The City of Prague

The seasons here in the city are perfect and that is one reason for the travelers to make a crowd there in the river banks. The river at the side of the city adds great beauty to the city and the climate of the city is perfect for tours and adventure in every aspect. The spring and the autumn time are discreet in this particular European city and thus travelers like to get there to the city in those times. More than the spring the city drives the tourists mostly in the month of the autumn, since the climate here at the city during that time remains ideal by all means. The summer time is great in the city and then also the weather remains pleasant, except the few days when the heat waves climb up the city. The Asian tourists like the weather of the city in the summer time in contrast to travelers from US and rest part of Europe. The most important time in the city is the winter. The UK and Australian people love the winter time in the city of castles, since the weather in the city remains perfect at that time. It is good to go to a walk on an autumn morning at the early sunrise, but the rainy days are more enjoyable in the city than anything.

Chapter 2. City Culture

The culture of the city is also strange and separate from that of rest of the European cities. The river here was the primary source of income at a particular time, but that is not the case now. The best thing in the city is the small community, which remains in fun with the beautiful music and amusement and even with the ultimate songs and art culture. Along with the communalist culture that is followed in the city, there is the importance of the chatty culture in the city. This is the culture that is quite different from that of the western culture. The people of the city are still influenced by the bohemian cult and that is best found among the inhabitants in the city. However the city is having the population derived from different parts of the world and that makes the sense for the modern mixed culture in the city. With such cultural differences there are several shopping locations which bloom with exclusive and fashionable items like Metropole Zličín, Centrum Chodov, ARTĚL Design Store, AVION Shopping Park which makes a shopaholic glued to these places.

Chapter 3. Food

The city is one of the biggest in the entire continent and one of the most densely populated cities even. The best thing in the city is the food habit and that is much different from rest part of Europe. The traditional food quality of the state and is less spicy and is different from that of the rest part of the nation. However the fascination for bakery is much more in the city and the most important thing is the inclusion of spice in the food habits. The food habit of the place has been influenced greatly influenced by the Asian and Latin American nations. There are many immigrants from those nations, and from there the Pakistan cuisine and Japanese cuisine has influenced the food habit to a great extent. The Brazilian foods and the Spanish spices along with Italian tasty cuisines have made the food culture of the city a perfect blend of bakery and spicy foods. However, the fascination for bakery has made the French burgers a delicious dish in the city.

There are numerous top restaurants and hotels in the city which highlighted the culture of the renovated city to a great height. Art deco imperial hotel, Prague Marriott hotel, Andel's hotel, The Mark Luxury hotel are some of the famous hotels in Prague known for their exquisite recipes and luxurious services at reasonable prices. In addition, the river based foods and the spice in them has made it quite elegant and delicious.

Chapter 4. Night Life

There are many top bars in the city like AAA exclusive club, K5 relax, Mecca club, DeJaVu Music Club & Bar, etc provide excellent entertainment for every kind of individuals. Furthermore, the different category of wine available in the city, and most importantly the night life in the city, being a modern intervention has been a great support for the travelers. Although the city is a big one, the count of night clubs and bars are much less, as compared to the other top cities in the continent. The main reason for that has been the influence of the bohemian cultures it is on extinction, but the effect of that is still best explained in the heritage and culture. The city has been one of the colorful cities of Europe and after the WWII the color sensibility of the city has been yet more. The golden towers and the heritage statues have made the city look like a golden one, although most of the castles and towers are renovated after the disaster made in the WWII. Red is another top color that is loved and liked by most of the inhabitants of the city.

Chapter 5. Experience The City of Prague

Prague is a city of varied history and known to the travelers as the "City of Thousand Spires" and it is a designated UNESCO world heritage site. Few years back, Prague was an unexplored destination for the travelers who were charting out the venues in the European cities. Now, it attracts and draws the maximum number of tourists from all over the world. Prague offers a century old long history and the centre of the city is compact. Here you will find the greatest architectures of the world resembling Renaissance, Gothic, Romanesque and Gothic style of architecture. There are abundant of richly designed palaces, beautiful parks and the most famous Czech made beer.

The Best Attractions of Prague

Charles Bridge

This bridge connects the two regions on the either side of the famous Vltava River. The bridge offers one of the best romantic views in between the either ends of the bridge. The entrance to the bridge from the two ends offers a picturesque view of the two towers Old

Town Bridge Tower and Lesser Town Bridge Tower. The view from the bridge offers a fairy tale glance of the city of Prague. Magnificent Prague Castle is seen from the bridge. The long view of the Vltava River also offers a delightful treat to most of the travelers embarking on this bridge.

Charles Bridge Museum

The history of the glorious river crossing is depicted in the famous Charles Bridge Museum. One can visit the Museum to know about the history of the old Charles Bridge of 14th century. The details and architectural information regarding the design and construction of bridge is exhibited in detail in this Museum. The replicas of the bridge in the form of small models are exhibited and the tools used to build the famous bridge are also presented inside the museum. The museum provides a lot of historical information about the artisans and architects of the ancient times. The construction of this bridge is shown in an attractive timeline.

Dancing House

This house is well known around the world for its unique design. The house is located along the side of the River Vltava. The design of the building will strike your eyes because it is the work of the modern architects amidst the historical buildings. The look of the house is slightly curvy and slanting at the floors and the ceilings. The house was built between 1992 and 1996. Only the top floor of the Dancing House is accessible by the tourists and it houses the city's most renowned restaurant: Ginger and Fred restaurant. From the top of this building sitting inside the restaurant, tourists can have a look at the beautiful colorful city.

Estates Theatre

This building is an example of the neo-classical genre built in the year 1783. This is the oldest theatre in Prague and regarded as the best theater in the European history. If you want to get the feel of the theatre, visit this theatre because you will get a special charm of the place where several directors, artists, musicians and playwright have spent most of their time. Those who appreciate western classical music, then this place are covered with the works of the famous composer Wolfgang Amadeus Mozart. The city of Prague and the Estates theatre had a great impact on the musical works of this famous composer.

Funicular Railway

This is a journey treat for the tourists travelling to Prague for a different kind of view around the city. It is a part of the Prague public transport network. The Funicular train travels from the Lesser Town to the hill top of Petrin. Travelling on board this train you can reach up the top of the Petrin hill where there is a huge garden. Amidst the garden there is the Petrin Observation Tower which is surrounded by a church a maze made of mirror. The observatory has many telescopes for the tourist to enjoy the distant view of the city from the top of the hill. The train has a single halt in the middle of the journey at Nebozizek Restaurant. Here the tourists can have a perfect dinner.

Golden Lane

Amidst the famous Prague castle region, the Golden Lane is a street with ancient heritage. The name of the street is popular because of the golden color which it exhibits during the day. The golden lane consists of several ancient houses and cottages. The street has its own divine beauty. This street is a delight for the tourists who want to see the natural reflection of the colors in the nature. All the houses are built during the medieval times and have texture made out of textiles. A certain amount is needed to enter this Golden Lane. Or you can take the help of the tour guide for the ease of roaming around d the streets.

Jewish Museum

The Jewish quarter has the best preserved Jewish historical monuments in a huge complex. The collection of the best monuments in Europe is located in the Jewish Museum. The tourists can purchase a ticket to enter the museum to glance at the beautiful historical monuments. One can see the presence of amazing synagogues such as the Jewish Ceremonial Hall and the Old Jewish Cemetery. If you buy a ticket of the Jewish Museum you can see the following monuments

Astronomical Clock

There are important things that you will find in the city and this is one of the most important attraction of the city. The tower has been built in the fourteenth century. The next important support that you can get in the city is one of the top features. This is one of the oldest clocks of the world. In fact this is one of the most perfect clocks of the world that gives near about perfect time. Thus do not miss the visit to this tower. The ultimate beauty of the tower is a great beauty. Its colorful and is one of the prime attraction of the city.

Jindrisska Tower

This tower was built in the Gothic era, built in 1472-1476. The gothic style is incorporated by the architect Mocker. This beautiful monument stands high at a height of 66m and is ten storied high. The tourists going at the top of the monument can have an amazing view of the city of Prague. From the tenth floor the tourists can look at the Wenceslas Square, National Museum and also at the magnificent Prague Castle. Inside the monument, the 6th floor has an exhibition gallery which displays of Prague Towers and a shop for souvenirs.

Prague castle

The castle is one of the most ancient one on the globe. The castle is one of the best one present today. It has been destroyed in the WWII, but government has renovated the castle that has been destroyed to 70%. The most important thing in the city has been the beauty of the old buildings. This castle has been built in 880 AD and hence is one of the oldest castles of the city. The beauty of the castle is one of the stunning sceneries of the world and thus considered the best in the city. The castle covers a wide area and the travelling time is near about 8 hours a day. The castle is one of the largest and most importantly, it is the only castle that has survived more than one world war. Learning the history of this castle will give you the chance to know the life of the people during the 880AD period.

Prague Zoo

The zoo of Prague is one of the best one in this world. There are altogether 5000 animals of 200 species of the world. The most important thing in the zoo is the variety of tigers and the different animals that are placed there in it. The support of the zoo is great and it is one the cheapest zoo in the world in terms of entry fee required to enter this zoo.

St. Vitus cathedral

This is one of the popular religious spot of the city. The major attraction of the castle is the looks of the place and this cathedral attracts large population of tourists every year. The architectural beauty of this cathedral will make any traveler spell bound. It is a great place to visit and is one of the oldest cathedrals in the entire European continent.

Vitava River

The river is one of the best spot in the city. The banks of the river are perfect. The ultimate thing that attracts the tourist towards this location is the river's natural spectacle. The bridge on the river has also been damaged in the world wars and has been renovated, since it is one of the top communicating zoneof the city. The best thing that the bridge in the river has given is the view of the city.

Wenceslas Square

This is another place where the night view is excellent. The great looks of the place is apparently wonderful. The city view from this place will make you spellbound. The night sky view and the lights in the city have made it a prime attraction for the tourists. The broad and the straight road in the middle of the city are great in looks and beauty. It is one of the popular business centers of the city. The most important part that counts is the number of visitors to this place. It can accommodate more than 40000 people at one time and that is a stunning thing in entire Europe.

Vysehrad Park and St. Peter & Paul Church

The most important support that the city looks can provide is this church and the club or the garden around it. If you are willing to get a look of the beauty of the medieval park, here is the ultimate look that you are going to experience. The great amusement park is having perfect looks and that is going to give the best experience for the tourists. The great and old looks may not provide vintage experience but will make you understand the reason behind the reputation impregnated by people on this magnificent city.

It is fact that there are few things in the city that are great and different from rest of the city sculptures. It is a city that is having most different looks and that made the city great for the tourists. They love to place for the glamour and the color and that is one reason why a tourist comes back to the city and goes through the city roads and the important city locations. The fantastic sculpture and the buildings has many outstanding features. The great looks that you will get from the city will surely attract you and you will have to get to the city again and again to find the nectar of the medieval and historical features in the state. The outlook of the city is medieval still now. Some of the Europeans say that the city is backward, but the city is having a great looks and that attracts the tourists to the spot. The great looks of the place has been a real attraction and the culture of the city is also quite different from that of the rest Europe. The city has been plundered in the world wars, but the perfect management of the government has restored its beauty to a great extent. This is the top thing that makes the sense of tourism.

Chapter 6. Shopping in The City

Shopping is another fantastic experience in the city. You will find numerous top plazas and shopping centers with outstanding fashionable garments and spices. The city shopping will also provide you the best looking arts and crafts, all made in bohemian style. They are unique in looks and outstanding in designs. However the fashion icon in the city has been the stars of the football team. You can find them often in the bars and the clubs and even in the shopping malls. The shopping malls are great to watch and fantastic to be seen. You can enjoy the shopping experience in this particular city of Europe in relaxed mood, since the location shows less attraction for traditional shopping. The superb spots for travel in the city are going to be cherishing and having a shopping experience with the travel is going to make your heart fulfilled. If you are going to the spit from Asia or from African nations, the bohemian castles and the ancient philosophical culture of the city is surely going to attract you. You will then simply love to do the shopping and have the beat nourishment from the trip. Palladium, Arkady Pankrac, Novy Simchov, Palac Flora, Myslbek Shopping Gallery,

Cerna Ruze, Slovansky dum, Vinohradsky Pavilon, Metropole Zlicin are some of the top shopping malls in the city of Prague. You will have a lot of fun and entertainment shopping at these shops. So, get ready with fully packed wallets.

Chapter 7. Places to Stay

Places for staying in this city are many and there are good numbers of top hotels available in the place starting from the 2 star hotels to 5 star ones. The most popular among those will accommodate you with cafe bar and pools even. Site seeing in the location is the top need and thus all the hotels provide a trip package for the tourists. The luxurious hotels even are less costly than you have expected, after visiting rest of the Europe. The economy of the place is perfect and is much lower than that of rest part of Europe. Along with the heritage travel spots, this place also is favored by the travelers, for the low cost features in it. The traditional hotels are even crafted beautifully and are great attraction for the tourists. The great beauty of the city has been great and that has been maintained even in a better way by the inhabitants of the place. The place is not that much popular for business summit as is for tourism. One reason for that is definitely the language bar, but among the Europeans, the city is preferred as a business meet location. The low cost of the city is often preferred by the companies in that continent. Here are a few top five star hotel in

Prague that you can try on your trip to this place. Hotel Paris Prague, Chateau Mcely Club Hotel and Forest retreat, Iron gate hotel and suites, The Mark Prague, Hotel General, Le Palais Art Hotel Prague, Four seasons Prague, InterContinental Praha, Boscolo Prague, Alchymist Grand Hotel and Spa, Corinthia Towers Hotel and many more.

Final Words

There are many important things in the state and the major ingredient in the city has been the ultimate looks and feel of the place. The lovely looking towers of the place and the beautiful devastation in the city have made the city elegant for the travelers. The most important thing in the city has been the escape game support. You have played any such games on your mobile devices and your PCs. Experience the game in real life in the city. This is the ultimate thing that you can get in the city. The place is a great one for shopping at cheaper rate and also for the colors. The city of colors is really a lovely one and is filled with different colors. Go to the clubs and you can also meet the locals. Palladium is a top place for shopping. Get there on the week days to avoid the crowds. Never miss the city view in the night sky and in the sunrise sky. The beauty of the city is totally different from that of the rest of Europe and that is a strong point in the city for sure. You will find the medieval looks back in Europe. Thus this city is going to give you an experience that is perfectly different from that of the other city looks. The city is out of sky scrapers, and the looks, even the roads are simply like that of the medieval Europe. So if you are not having a proper idea about Europe in the medieval time, get to Prague and enjoy the beauty of the city.

The city has beautiful designs and perfect looking visiting spots. The great culture of the city along with the wonderful structures has made the city great and that is the most interesting thing in the place. There are numerous visiting spots in the place and that has created many attractive places for the tourism. The important fact is that most of the places are built centuries back, but that are maintained still now. Much of the towers have been destroyed in the WWII, but that are renovated by the government and the castles are brought back to the original looks once again. The astronomical clocks and the castles are mounted with the perfect colors to make the city filled with colors. The bohemian culture is still there in the city and that made the city full of light and color. The enigmatic beauty of the city and the city castle from the river bank and the bridge middle makes the city look like a medieval gift to the world. The Bohemians are out of the city, but their cultures and their preferences are still there in the corners of the city and that made the city even more beautiful. This is one of the cities in Europe, where there are rickshaw still plying and that is one of the cheapest cities in the entire continent. The most important fact of the city is the great food habit of them.

The hospitality of the people in this city, will surely going to impress the visitors to this destination. The environment and the overall beauty of this city will make the trip of any traveler memorable for lifetime. This city is visited by large number of people every year.

Thank You Page

I want to personally thank you for reading my book. I hope you found information in this book useful and I would be very grateful if you could leave your honest review about this book. I certainly want to thank you in advance for doing this.

If you have the time, you can check my other books too.

www.ingramcontent.com/pod-product-compliance
Lightning Source LLC
LaVergne TN
LVHW021747060526
838200LV00052B/3521